MICROBIOLOGY

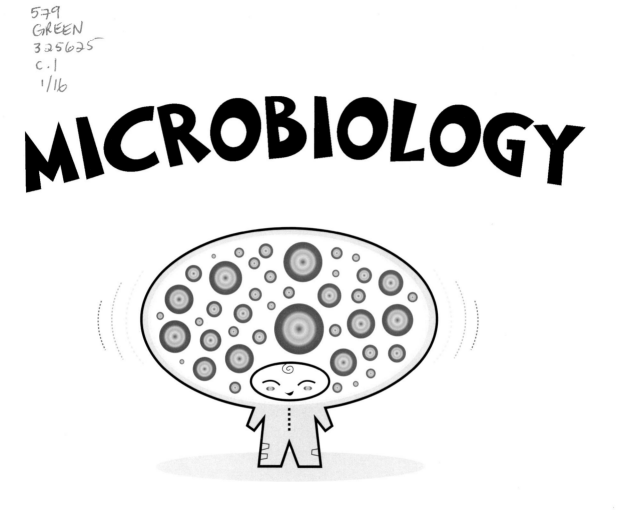

KINGFISHER

NEW YORK

KINGFISHER
LONDON & NEW YORK

Published in the United States by Kingfisher
175 Fifth Ave., New York, NY 10010
Kingfisher is an imprint of Pan Macmillan

Consultants: Professor Timothy D. McHugh (University College London) and Ian Armitage
Designed and created by Basher
www.basherbooks.com
Text written by Dan Green

Thanks to everyone at Toucan, Kingfisher and Macmillan who have been part
of the Basher science series, including Ellen, Dan, Anna, Mary, Adrian, Melissa,
Martina, Angus, Belinda, Russell, Catherine, Jane, Lisa, Carol and Marion.
Dedicated to all the students, parents, teachers, stores, and librarians who have
supported the books.

Distributed in the U.S. and Canada by Macmillan, 75 Fifth Ave., New York, NY 10010

Library of Congress Cataloging-in-Publication Data
has been applied for

ISBN 978-0-7534-7195-1 (HC)
ISBN 978-0-7534-7194-4 (PB)

Kingfisher books are available for special promotions and premiums.
For details contact: Special Markets Department, Macmillan,
175 Fifth Ave., New York, NY 10010.

For more information, please visit www.kingfisherbooks.com

Printed in China
9 8 7 6 5 4 3 2 1
1TR/0115/WKT/UG/128MA

CONTENTS

Introduction

When it comes to organisms, we humans are not typical. In fact, most of the critters that count as "living things" are weird, strange, and unusual. The bulk of life on this planet goes on out of sight, hidden from view in the realm of microscopic single-celled organisms. There are more bacteria than there are stars in the universe and more microbugs in a pinch of soil than there are people on the planet. Our bodies are microbe jungles. These teeny-tiny tykes can cause disease, spoil food, rot our teeth, and make water unhealthy. They lurk in our kitchens and bathrooms and attack us in hospitals. But they also provide the planet with oxygen, help plants grow, digest organic waste, and help our bodies function.

The first person to look into this hidden world was the Dutch textile merchant Antonie van Leeuwenhoek. In the 1670s he peered through his hand lens and was amazed to see tiny wriggling "animalcules." New species of bacteria are still being discovered today, and there is such a dizzying diversity of these cavorting beasties that we don't yet know half of what they can do.

Antonie van Leeuwenhoek

Chapter 1
Microbugs

It may look as if big hairy animals—elephants, polar bears, your teacher—rule the planet, but we don't live in the Age of Mammals. No, we live in the Age of Bacteria. Smaller than the eye can see, there are more bacteria in your mouth than there are people on Earth! These life forms are unbreakable—they can survive in the roughest, toughest places and have already outlasted humans by millions of years. Other Microbugs include Bacteria's cousins the archaea, strange stripped-down viruses, blobby protists, and microscopic members of the fungi and algae families. Let's see what they have to say.

Bacteria

Archaea

Protists

Microfungus

Microphytes

Virus

Pandoravirus

Bacteria
Microbugs

* Single-celled microbes that include both good and bad germs
* Bacteria are "prokaryotes" (say *pro-carrie-yotes*)
* The cells of prokaryotes lack a nucleus to contain their genome

We may be very small, but we demand respect! Earth belongs to us. We were here before you animals evolved, and we'll survive long after you're gone. You'll find us everywhere—in clouds and oceans, soil and rivers, and in every living thing. We outnumber you. Why, your own body has far more of us than it has human cells!

Some of us are really nasty and make you sick (and smell bad!), but most of us are good and quietly help you make vitamins and digest food in your stomach. We make foods such as Bug Buddy Yogurt, and we're useful in breaking down poop in sewers and clearing toxic waste and oil spills. As cyanobacteria, we help plants feed and use sunlight to produce oxygen from carbon dioxide. You couldn't live without us!

* Discovered: 1676 (Antonie van Leeuwenhoek)
* Typical size: 0.00002–0.0002 in. (0.0005–0.005mm)
* Estimated number of bacteria on Earth: five thousand billion billion billion

Bacteria

Archaea
Microbugs

☀ Single-celled microbes but genetically distinct from bacteria
☀ Prokaryotes that have been around for at least 3.5 billion years
☀ Archaea represent a major—and vital—part of life on Earth

Don't listen to boastful Bacteria—we were here first! To survive this long, you've gotta be tough. We hang out in the deepest rocks and oceans, we chill out inside nuclear waste tanks, and thrive in hot mud, salt lakes, and deadly acid. We can endure crushing pressures and icy cold.

We like to feed on amazing stuff such as sulfur, ammonia, and hydrogen gas. Some of us obtain energy from sunlight, but without releasing oxygen, unlike Cyanobacteria. Others live in human and animal guts, helping cows digest grass (which unfortunately produces a lot of that smelly greenhouse gas methane). We are also handy in sewage treatment. It is from us toughies that scientists get useful enzymes that can withstand heat, acids, and alkalis. And, unlike *some* Bacteria, we don't cause disease!

● Typical size: 0.000004–0.00059 in. (0.0001–0.015mm)
● Kingdom of Archaea created: 1977 (Carl Woese and George E. Fox)
● Deepest living archaean: 6.78 mi. (10.911km) (Mariana Trench, Pacific Ocean)

Archaea

Protists
Microbugs

* ✴ Protists are ancient, single-celled microorganisms
* ✴ They are "eukaryotes" (say *you-carrie-yotes*)
* ✴ The genomes of a eukaryote are found in the cell's nucleus

We do our own thing, but don't confuse us with Bacteria and Archaea. No, we are eukaryotes—just like you—and evolved when some bacteria pooled their resources, teaming up inside a single cell. Modern plants, animals, and fungi are our relatives, yet we are something "other." Our members include algae, amoebas, and Slime Mold.

We live anywhere there's liquid water and are not a bad lot, on the whole. Many of us eat Bacteria and make water safe for drinking (so don't upset us—or the environment—by flushing too much disinfectant). There are some evil beasties among us, though, such as deadly *Plasmodium* and *Toxoplasma gondii* (you'll meet them later). One of us feeds on bacteria but switches to eating brains when it gets inside a human. Ew! How's that for something else?

* ● Kingdom of "Protista" proposed: 1866 (Ernst Haeckel)
* ● Deadliest protist-caused disease: malaria, killing one million people per year
* ● Number of deaths from brain-eating *Naegleria fowleri*: 132 (U.S.: 1962–2013)

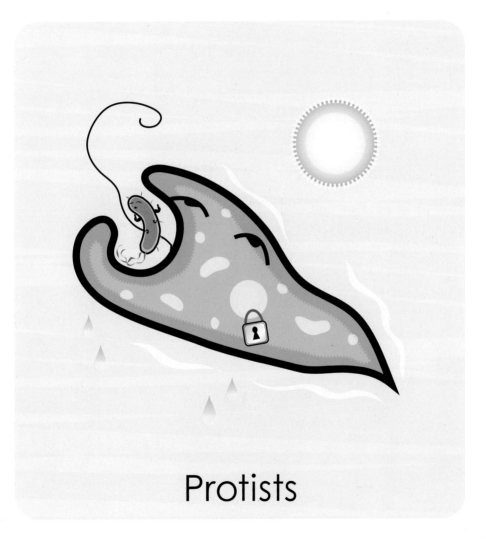

Protists

Microfungus
Microbugs

✳ Tiny mold and mildew that do not produce fruiting bodies
✳ This "no-fun-guy" spoils fruit and spreads across bread
✳ *Penicillium* is a lifesaving microfungus that kills nasty bacteria

I'm a moldy critter whose tiny spores spread through soil, wind, and water to engulf plants and cling to hair and skin (think athlete's foot). I have also been known to kill off the mighty elm tree. There is some good in me, though. As Yeast, I help bread rise and I'm the "blue" in stinky blue cheese (well, some people like it). I also team up with algae to form lichen.

Microfungus

● No. of microfungi species: around 56,000
● No. of Roquefort blue cheeses made: 3 million per year, 20,750 tons (18,824 tonnes)
● Discovery of Dutch elm disease microfungus: 1921 (Bea Schwarz)

14

Microphytes

Microbugs

* Microscopic algae that live singly or join together in long chains
* These "miniplants" have no roots, stems, or leaves
* In the sea, they produce oxygen and suck up carbon dioxide

Microphytes

Come on in—the water's lovely! We bob around in marine and fresh water. Each of us has only one cell to speak of, but we are awesomely important. The basic foodstuff of sea creatures such as clams and oysters, we single-handedly keep thousands of species alive. We also produce about half of the oxygen in the atmosphere and break down nasty carbon dioxide.

● Typical size: 0.00004–0.00394 in. (0.001–0.1mm)
● Estimated number of species: 200,000–800,000
● CO_2 removed from atmosphere by microphytes: 11 billion tons (10 bn tonnes) /year

Virus
Microbugs

✳ A rogue packet of DNA or RNA in a protective protein coating
✳ This itty-bitty critter can spell bad news for some living things
✳ Can also be good and contributes to Earth's genetic diversity

Lacking the biological machinery to reproduce, I transfer my genetic material into living cells. I "hijack" their workings and trick them into producing copies of me. I infect plants and fungi as well as animals. As Bug Buddy Bacteriophage, I can even get inside (and kill) Bacteria.

I'm known for causing yucky illnesses such as chickenpox, the common cold, messy diarrhea, and spouting vomit. Worse still, in cases of influenza, measles, HIV, and some cancers, I can be fatal. I am not affected by antibiotics, but vaccines can help you produce antibodies to block my tricks. They even made my smallpox-causing relative extinct. I have my uses, too. I encourage natural recycling by killing bacteria and toxic algae in oceans. Plus, scientists use my gene-hacking skills to transfer genes from one cell to another.

● Typical size: 0.0000000008–0.00000001 in. (0.00000002–0.0000003mm)
● Discovered: 1898 (tobacco mosaic virus, Martinus Beijerinck)
● Viruses in a teaspoon of seawater: about one million

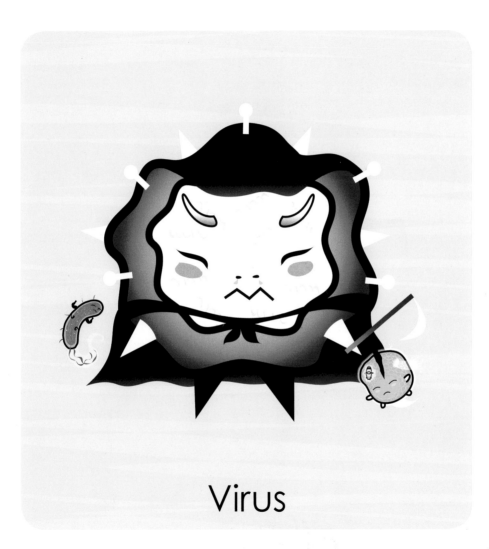

Virus

Pandoravirus
Microbugs

✳ A giant virus with chunky genomes and numerous genes
✳ Harmless to humans, it infiltrates and infects amoeba
✳ Could be the missing link between cells and viruses

I'm a maxi meanie, the biggest virus ever found. Who'd have thought that something as big as me would be good at hiding? Well, I remained undiscovered until 2013, when I was unearthed in lakes and on beaches. Like Pandora's box in the old story, I have opened up a new world for scientists . . . but is it good or bad?

I'm a shapeless specter. In fact, I'm so blobby that I've been mistaken for a bacterium. I'm virus through and through, however. While my pal Virus spends a lot of effort safecracking animal cells and Bug Buddy Bacteriophage breaks into Bacteria, I get my kicks by opening up amoeba. I reprogram Protists' cells to make copies of my genetic information and I make 'em work hard. You see, I've got a much bigger genome than most viruses. I'm truly "XL"-ent!

● Discovery: 2013 (Jean-Michel Claverie and Chantal Abergel)
● Typical size: 0.00006 in. (0.0015mm) long; 0.00002 in. (0.0005mm) wide
● Number of genes: up to 2,500 (HIV has 10–12)

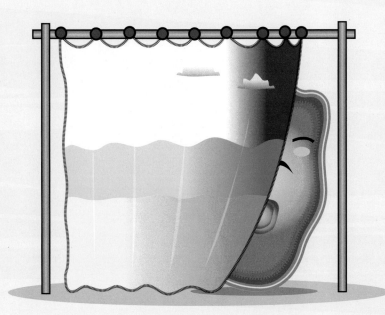

Pandoravirus

Chapter 2
Bacteria Basics

Bacteria are rugged, rough-and-tumble life forms. Uncomplicated, yes, but their design is hard to beat. The walls of their single cells are rigid and made of a polymer that is not found anywhere else in nature. Whiz them in a blender and they still come out unharmed! They are so adaptable that they inhabit every environment on planet Earth. Although singletons, Bacteria coordinate their behavior by "counting" their numbers and acting when they hit a critical mass. Should a catastrophe hit the planet, near-indestructible Endospore would repopulate the place.

Cell

Bacterial Growth

Autotroph

Heterotroph

Aerobe

Anaerobe

Movement

Communication

Population

Community

Symbiont

Parasite

Biofilm

Endospore

Cell
▪ Bacteria Basics

* ❋ The most basic unit of all living things
* ❋ Makes the essential chemical components for life
* ❋ New cells are made when old cells divide in two

I am the smallest living thing. I make up every bacterium, protist, fungus, plant, and animal. A human body is multicellular—about 100 trillion of me form your different body parts. A bacterium has only a single cell.

I'm basically a bag of watery chemicals that includes DNA. The DNA provides a blueprint for making proteins and controlling how the cell functions. It's copied and passed to the next generation when I divide. In eukaryotic cells (Protists, Microfungus) DNA is protected in a nucleus within the cytoplasm. In prokaryotic cells (Bacteria, Archaea) DNA has no protecting nucleus. Bacterial cells come in several shapes—balls, rods, spirals, or wispy strands. They also have short stretches of DNA that they can swap between each other. We're "cell-sational"!

* ● Discovery of cells: 1665 (Robert Hooke)
* ● Typical size of a prokaryotic cell: 0.00039–0.0039 in. (0.001–0.01mm)
* ● Typical size of eukaryotic (human) cell: 0.0008 in. (0.02mm)

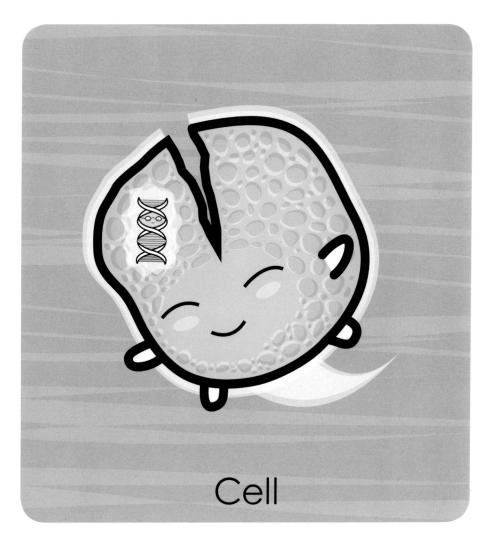

Cell

Bacterial Growth
Bacteria Basics

☀ This is an increase in the number of cells—not their size
☀ Bacteria reproduce by simple division of the cell into two
☀ This takeover artiste multiplies by exponential increase

I'm infection perfection. The life of a bacterial cell is uncomplicated. It is simply a case of reproducing as quickly as possible to take advantage of available nutrients. I let Cell expand to twice its size and then split it down the middle to produce two cells.

Under this "grow and divide" regime, one cell makes two; two become four; four become eight; and so on. This means I rapidly spread infection. I have four phases. In the "lag phase," I bide my time, preparing to strike. In the "log phase," my cell numbers increase exponentially, doubling with each division. Decreasing food and oxygen slow my expansion. In this "stationary phase," I get smaller and begin to make my own food. Last comes the "death phase." Well, all things must pass!

● Rate of *E. coli* cell division: once every 20 minutes
● Number of new *E. coli* cells in one day: 2,500 billion billion (in ideal conditions)
● Slowed by chilling; usually stopped by freezing

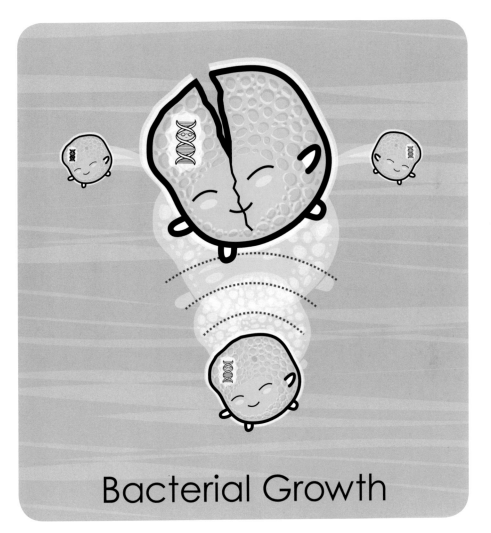

Bacterial Growth

Autotroph
Bacteria Basics

* Self-feeding living things that make their own food
* Many make food from chemicals in their environment
* Autotrophs provide food for other living things (heterotrophs)

I'm the producer. I kick-start things and foot the bill for life on Earth. Not to make too much fuss about it, but without me you'd all perish pretty quickly! You see, I take "dead" chemicals and turn them into living food.

Some autotrophs use photosynthesis. They use light energy to convert inorganic chemicals, such as carbon dioxide and water, into nutritious organic chemical sugars, fats, and proteins. Other autotrophs use chemosynthesis, obtaining energy by breaking down inorganic chemicals. Archaea mastered this trick early on, surviving on the flow of chemicals from deep-sea vents. Later you'll meet Cyanobacteria, who soaks up sunlight to produce oxygen. And all the time I put this work in, Heterotroph scarfs my ready-made food. It's so unfair!

● Chemosynthesis first proposed: 1890 (Sergei Nikolaevich Vinogradskii)
● First chemosynthetic organism discovered: 1980 (Colleen Cavanaugh)
● First known cyanobacteria: c. 1.5 billion years ago

Autotroph

Heterotroph
Bacteria Basics

☀ These dudes cannot make their own food
☀ Their food comes from autotrophs or other heterotrophs
☀ They range from unicellular bacteria to multicellular animals

I'm the great consumer. Unlike Autotroph, I'm not big on building food out of sunshine and chemicals. I'm a fast-food fan on a "see-food" diet—I see food and I eat it! Gulp!

Like all living things, I need carbon to construct my body and keep it running. I get it ready-made from Autotroph by breaking down its organic chemicals into simpler constituents. Autotroph may keep the whole show on the road, sure, but what a dull place it would be without me—I'm talking lions and starfish, grizzlies and mushrooms. As well as plant-nibbling and meat-munching animals, my number includes many single-celled bacteria. These minimarvels perform a vital function—they live on the products and remains of organic things, decomposing waste. That's right, it's me that stops the planet from drowning in its own filth.

● Percentage of living things that are heterotrophs: 95%
● Most prokaryotes and all fungi are heterotrophs
● First known nitrogen-fixing heterotroph bacteria: 1889 (*Rhizobium leguminosarum*)

Heterotroph

Aerobe
■ Bacteria Basics

✳ An "air-breathing" microbe that lives in an oxygen atmosphere
✳ Uses reactive oxygen to break down sugars for energy
✳ Some aerobes can survive without oxygen for a short time

Work it, baby! A bacterium needs to care for its metabolism, and I thrive and survive in an oxygen-rich atmosphere. "Metabolism" is a fancy term for the way all living things change chemicals to get energy and feed themselves.

Microbes have many ways of getting food. They are small and must absorb molecules from their environment. They break them down to release energy and create smaller molecules that they can use for nutrition. Aerobic bacteria use the powerful gas oxygen to split (oxidize) molecules of sugar or fat. This releases energy, usually with carbon dioxide and water. This trick is something that all cells of living creatures can do. I'm easy to find—put me in a test tube of broth and I'll migrate toward the gassy oxygen at the surface. Hubble bubble!

● "Obligate" aerobes: absolutely require oxygen to survive
● All animals, most fungi, and some bacteria are obligate aerobes
● Example of an obligate aerobe: *Myobacterium tuberculosis*

Aerobe

Anaerobe
Bacteria Basics

* A type of microbe that can survive without oxygen
* Most anaerobes are bacteria, and many live in our gut
* Anaerobic bacteria are found buried in mud and deep water

I'm Captain Stinkypants. I'm a bacterial garbage collector and a noxious, bubbling bottomfeeder. Without me you would soon be choking on your own filth and waste.

Unlike Aerobe, my metabolism isn't tied to oxygen. There are three types of me: oxygen is poison for "obligate" anaerobes; "aerotolerant" microbes can live in both oxygen-free and airy environments; and "facultative" anaerobes are actually aerobic microbes that can live without oxygen in times of shortage. I lurk at the base of the barrel, at the bottom of ponds, and in thick, black muds. As well as fermenting beer, I treat raw sewage and decompose the remains of plants. When this is done without oxygen and compressed over million of years, oil and coal are produced. I'm tiny, yes, but powerful.

● Anaerobic digestion: used to generate biogas
● First anaerobic digester: 1859 (Mumbai, India)
● Temperature of anaerobic digestion tanks: 86–36 °F (30–58 °C)

Anaerobe

Movement
■ Bacteria Basics

✳ Many bacteria use one or more whippy "flagella" to move
✳ They move to find food and avoid danger (and their own waste)
✳ They also respond to temperature, light, and gravity by moving

I really get a wiggle on! When I'm around, a bacterium's fine flagella whir in a corkscrew motion, powering Cell along like an outboard motor. Way to go!

When a bacterium has many flagella, they can wind together to create a chunky paddle that makes Cell "run" hotfoot away from harm or toward food. Rotating clockwise, the fibers unwind to form crazy waggling hair that sends Cell "tumbling" wildly—useful for finding goodies in the environment quickly. "Gliding" is the mysterious way in which bacteria move across surfaces. *E. coli*, whom you'll meet later, has a lot of flagella on its surface to whip it from place to place. It swims like a fish, traveling at up to 100 cell lengths per second—that's faster than a cheetah runs relative to its body length!

● Movement types: random tumbling, direct running, and gliding
● Speed of whipping movement: 200–1000 revs per minute
● Typical flagellum size: 0.0000008 in. (0.00002mm) wide x 0.00059–0.00079 (0.015–0.02) long

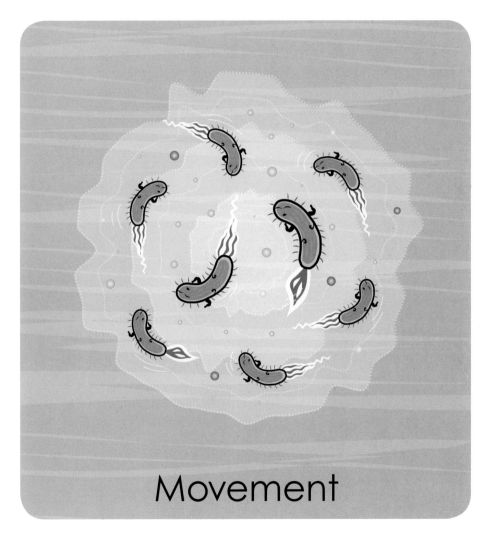

Movement

Communication

■ Bacteria Basics

☀ Bacteria communicate by a mode called "quorum sensing"
☀ In this way they sense their population density (crowding)
☀ This allows bacteria to coordinate their group behavior

If you think those Microbugs called Bacteria are just dumb cells, think again! Thanks to me, they produce "signal molecules" that they can pick up, keep under watch, and use to "count" their numbers. This makes them great communicators.

When Community is small, these signals are ignored. But as the number of Bacteria increases, so too does the concentration of signal molecules. That's my way of telling Bacteria that they've gotta change their behavior. And they do . . . all at the same time! This can mean turning on bioluminescent lights in a coordinated display, releasing toxins, or inducing disease. Certain bacteria even share a "trade language," which enables them to count both their own numbers and those of other species.

● Quorum sensing first observed: 1981 (*Vibrio fischeri* in bioluminescent squid)
● Concentration of *V. fischeri* in seawater: 2,840 per fl. oz. (100 per mL)
● Lowest concentration of *V. fischeri* in squid light organs: 284 bn fl. oz. (10 bn /mL)

Communication

Population
■ Bacteria Basics

✳ A count of the numbers of a single species of bacteria
✳ Single-species populations are called "pure cultures"
✳ Multispecies populations are called "communities"

I am The Count—the numbers guy who tells you how many bacteria of a particular species are around, either in a single-species sisterhood or as part of multispecies Community (such as *E. coli* in Gut Flora, for example).

I grow and shrink in response to the food in my immediate environment. If there are a lot of nutrients, my Bacteria get busy dividing to increase their number. As you already know, my Bacteria Basics buddy Communication lets individuals know how to behave. For example, under attack from other populations, my bacteria release toxins to defend themselves. Or they might turn on the toxins to attack others. And whenever food starts to run low, Movement helps me trundle off to find better feeding grounds or to build Endospore's escape capsules.

● Size of petri dish for growing bacterial cultures: 100 mm (large)
● Melting point of agar culturing gel: around 185 °F (85 °C)
● Invention of agar culturing gel: 1882 (Fanny Angelina Eilshemius)

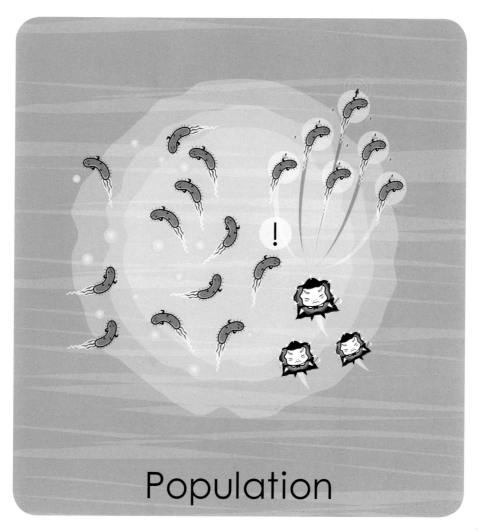

Population

Community
Bacteria Basics

* Several populations living together in the same environment
* Sometimes populations are "antagonistic" to each other
* At other times populations cooperate or communicate

I'm a bacterial city. I'm what happens when two or more populations of bacterial species live side by side. Human cities are made up of single species. My metropolis is like having giraffes, swans, snakes, and fish as neighbors. I've sure got the community spirit.

For you humans, the microbial communities closest to home are the bugs that thrive on your skin, in your mouth, and in your gut. Different populations may compete for resources, but they survive more easily if their resources are different. Speedy reactions are key—reproducing quickly when food is plentiful and shutting down when times get tough. Endospore can tell you about *that*. The dirty tricks and toxins of one species make life hard for another, and this helps keep nasty bugs out of your gut (well, mostly).

- Average number of bacterial species in mouth: 100–200
- Average number of bacteria on a clean tooth: 1,000–100,000
- Average number of bacteria on an unbrushed tooth: 100 million–1 billion

Community

Symbiont
■ Bacteria Basics

✳ An organism that lives alongside different organisms
✳ The relationship may be mutually beneficial or one-sided
✳ Many animals have gut bacteria that aid digestion

Life is so sweet when we just live together, no? Call me an old hippie but, hey, cooperation is the name of the game! You scratch my back and I'll scratch yours.

Bacteria have a bad rep for causing diseases, but I'm one bug that just loves to help in any way I can. Take gut bacteria, for example. They help you deal with tricky foods such as fiber and lactose, and they make meals more digestible. Some gut bacteria even compete against others to knock nasty bugs out of action. And what about the dudes that help plants get a "fix" of nitrogen from soil? These are *good guys*! I come in two types. The commensals get the perks but don't return the favor, while the mutualists benefit both partners. Trouble is, my nasty cousin, Parasite, sees things very differently . . .

● Discovery of symbiosis: 1869 (Anton de Bary)
● "Commensal": one organism benefits; the other is neither harmed nor benefits
● "Mutualistic": both partners benefit

Symbiont

Parasite

◼ Bacteria Basics

✳ A symbiont that harms its host, usually without killing it
✳ Parasites include helminths, protists, viruses, fungi, and bacteria
✳ Malaria is caused by the *Plasmodium* parasite

I am the unwelcome guest, and *you* may be my host!
A prince of pestilence, I have been bringing down
people and animals for millions of years. As long as there
have been cellular hosts, I have been crashing the party.

You see, not all symbionts are friendly. I live alongside other
organisms, but instead of helping them, I hijack them. This
is no two-way street, believe me. All I'm interested in is
completing my life cycle. I try not to kill my hosts—I'd be
homeless, after all—but I don't mind if I trash the place.
I can even change my host's behavior to stack the odds
in my favor. Just wait until you hear what *Toxoplasma
gondii* has to say about that! In my defense, I'd say that
if my host manages to adapt over time, we may evolve
to become a mutualistic team. But let's wait and see.

● Endoparasite: enters the body through the skin, in the air, or in food and drink
● Ectoparasite: stays on the outside (for example, a flea)
● Vector: something that transmits a disease or parasite (for example, a mosquito)

Parasite

Biofilm
■ Bacteria Basics

☀ A slimy mat of microbes that stick together on wet surfaces
☀ May contain one species or many different species of microbes
☀ It forms by communication between the microbial cells

Call me shallow if you like—it's all about surfaces with me: on rocks in streams, from hot springs to glaciers, in pipes and showers, on boat hulls and teeth. I'm one slimy sucker!

A chemical signal calls all free-swimming bacteria to gather on a surface. At first, they cling together any way they can. Then they start producing a thick slime that gloops them together—that's me! I protect the microbes from the outside—detergents and antibiotics are futile. I am difficult to remove, which means I can cause chronic infections in the body, such as those that occur in the lungs of cystic fibrosis sufferers. I form tooth-rotting plaque. I have an ability to swap genetic material, which means I can quickly transfer antibiotic immunity from cell to cell. I simply hunker down and "stick" it out!

● Biofilm thickness: 0.00008–19.68 in. (0.002–500mm)
● Number of species in a dental biofilm: up to 1,000
● Time it takes for plaque to harden: 48 hours

Biofilm

Endospore
■ Bacteria Basics

✳ A dormant form of a bacterium awaiting regeneration
✳ The process of making an endospore is driven by starvation
✳ Special measures are needed to destroy endospores

Think you'll get rid of me? I'm bombproof! A supertough armored container for a bacterium, I'm built to last. Like a time capsule, I bundle up my genetic information and keep it unharmed for an eternity.

I'm almost impervious to heat, cold, and radiation. I can stay buried under ice for thousands of years and survive forest fires. I can even travel across space. And all of this without needing a scrap of food! When Community is on the verge of starvation, word goes out (via "quorum sensing") to form me. A bacterium duplicates its genetic material, but instead of dividing and splitting as normal, it encloses the new copy in a tough, double-thick cell wall. Only "firmicute" bacteria can do this—firm, yes; cute, not always. I may starve, but I will return. Mwahaha!

● Oldest endospores revived: up to 40 million years old
● First disease-causing bacteria identified: 1877 ("anthrax"—*Bacillus anthrasis*)
● 2001 anthrax attack: 22 people fell ill after contact with anthrax endospores

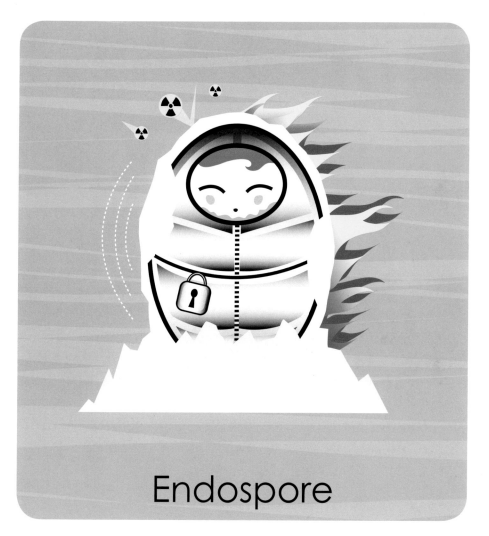

Endospore

Chapter 3
Body Battlers

Your body is under constant attack. A renegade army of expert infiltrators and highly dangerous hit men are all trying to take up residence inside your body—from that peevish protist, the malaria-causing *Plasmodium*, to the bacterial bruiser *Mycobacterium tuberculosis*. But your body has its own crack team of Body Battlers who put up a fight on your behalf. These heroes include your body's White Blood Cell surveillance and defense forces, gooey Goblet Cells and Ciliate Cells, and your own onboard bacterial cargo of Bug Buddies. Battle stations!

Red Blood Cell

Plasmodium

White Blood Cells

HIV

Macrophage

Mycobacterium tuberculosis

Goblet Cell

Ciliate Cell

Helminth

Gut Flora

Streptococcus

E. coli

Red Blood Cell
■ Body Battlers

✳ Donut-shaped cell that carries oxygen around the body
✳ Its red color comes from iron-rich hemoglobin
✳ Vulnerable to attack from malaria-causing *Plasmodium*

Rough and "reddy," I am the raw material that carries life-giving oxygen (O_2) in the blood. I take O_2 to Cell to use as fuel for the chemical reactions that keep the body going. You could say I'm a breath of fresh air!

My secret ingredient is an iron-rich chemical called hemoglobin (say *hee-moh-glow-bin*), which picks up O_2 as blood travels through the lungs. Normally, after about 120 days of toting O_2 around the body, I'm finished. I get broken down and flushed out of the body in urine. (It's me that makes your pee look yellow!) There are times when blood is infected by Body Battler *Plasmodium*—a parasite that causes a killer disease called malaria. It gets inside me and rips me open. I'm left to drift like a broken plastic bag and am no longer able to carry oxygen.

● Discovered: 1658 (Jan Swammerdam)
● Typical size: 0.0003 in. (0.007mm)
● Number of red blood cells in one drop of blood: more than five million

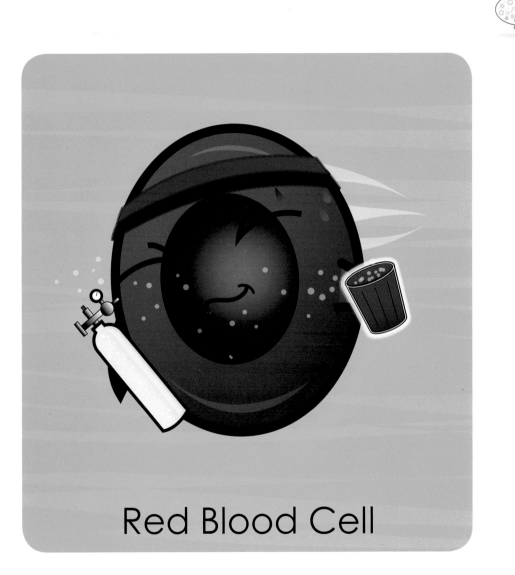

Red Blood Cell

Plasmodium

Body Battlers

* This parasite targets red blood cells and liver cells
* Causes an illness called malaria
* Malaria is transmitted by certain types of mosquitoes

Zzzzzzzz! That high-pitched whine is the sound of doom approaching. I'm a tiny tropical terror that slips into the skin with a mosquito bite. Deadly, sneaky, and my life cycle is complex and full of tricks. I sure get a "buzz" out of this!

My first disguise (a wriggly "sporozoite") gets me into a body's liver cells, where my nucleus copies itself over and over again to make an army of "merozoites." Several days later this army makes straight for the bloodstream, where it attacks Red Blood Cell. Ripping through millions of those oxygen-carrying critters, my army makes a person suffer attacks of burning fever, deep chills, and shuddering sweats—malaria! Losing too many red blood cells can be fatal. Medication, mosquito nets, insecticides, and controlling standing water are helping humans fight back.

● Discovered: 1885 (Ettore Marchiafava, Angelo Celli)
● Transmitted by: infected female *Anopheles* mosquitoes
● Number of species of malaria-transmitting *Anopheles* mosquitoes: 20

Plasmodium

White Blood Cells
Body Battlers

* Roving blood cells that help keep a body healthy
* Form part of a body's immune system
* These guys are known officially as leukocytes

Who's in control here? Found alongside Red Blood Cell in blood (in much smaller numbers), White Blood Cells (WBCs) monitor the highways and byways of the body. We put a stop to any threat entering uninvited. Let's meet the crew.

Neutrophils (say *new-trow-fills*) target bacteria and fungi invaders. Eosinophils (*eyo-sin-no-fills*) are parasite-busters. Basophils (*bas-oh-fills*) are alert to allergies, while monocytes (*mon-noh-sites*) mop up and lymphocytes (*lim-foh-sites*) kill off body-cells-gone-bad. Collectively, we have a training regime that teaches us to recognize the enemy and hone our killing techniques. Until an "autoimmune disease" such as HIV shows up, that is. That Body Battler makes us fight one another, mistaking our own kind for invaders and weakening the body's defensive shield.

● Number of WBCs in a human body: 20–55 billion
● Blood make-up: 54.3% (plasma); 45% (RBC); 0.7% (WBC)
● Breakdown: neutro. (65%), lympho. (25%), mono. (6%), eosino. (4%), baso. (1%)

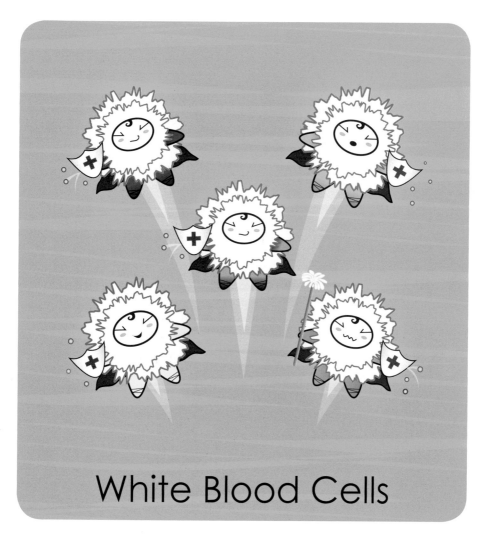

White Blood Cells

HIV
■ Body Battlers

☀ A tiny virus that looks like a round capsule covered in spikes
☀ HIV stands for "human immunodeficiency virus"
☀ This killer disease weakens the body's self-defense system

I'm a ball of badness. People who have me in their body are "HIV-positive," but there's nothing positive about me, I can tell you! I lay waste to the body's immune system by attacking the very defense forces striving to keep a person safe from invaders like me. How mean is that?

I sneak inside White Blood Cells known as lymphocytes. To start with, a person feels like they have a bad cold, but I stick around for 7 to 11 years, attacking the body's immune system. Eventually, the person's WBC count is so low that he or she can no longer keep the body safe from disease. HIV is transmitted by direct contact with bodily fluids, such as blood—you can't just catch it in the air or by holding hands. As yet, there's no cure for me, although there are drugs that slow my progress.

● Discovered: 1983 (Luc Montagnier, Anthony Gallo)
● Number of people living with HIV: 33.4 million (2014)
● Number of HIV-related deaths (from AIDS): two million per year (2014)

HIV

Macrophage
■ Body Battlers

✳ The body's first line of defense against infection
✳ A type of white blood cell (WBC) that gives long-term immunity
✳ Comes from monocytes stored in the spleen

I'm a big eater with a healthy appetite—call me Jumbo. When invaders come knocking, I gobble 'em up. I surround, engulf, and digest all kinds of nasty microbes, including *Mycobacterium tuberculosis*. I can even shoot arms out of my sides to pull those uglies into my wobbly embrace.

While the rest of the WBC crew mobilize in emergencies, I'm here for the long haul. I've got a good memory, too. Once I've encountered and defeated a certain intruder, I never forget it—nor how to fight it. This skill helps build up long-term immunity. When a pathogen (something that causes disease) gets into a body for the first time, it can make a person very sick. But once I learn how to neutralize the threat, details are stored, ready for access should that particular bad guy ever show up again.

● Discovered: 1882 (Ilya Mechnikov)
● Typical size: 0.00083 in. (0.021mm)
● Number of "phagocyte" cells in 1 pt. of human blood: 2.84 billion (6 billion/L)

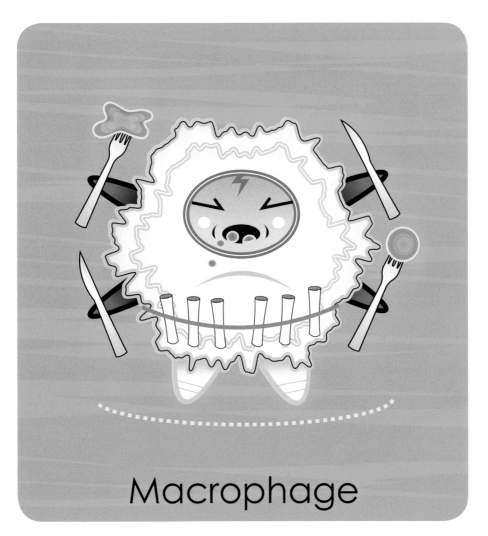

Macrophage

Mycobacterium tuberculosis

Body Battlers

* A rod-shaped bacterium with a thick, waxy wall
* This airborne germ causes a potentially fatal disease
* Takes up residence in the lungs, causing breathing problems

Yo! I am the bringer of tuberculosis—TB for short. This grisly lung disease causes chest pains, weight loss, chills, night sweats, and hackin' and coughin' all the way to the coffin!

I'm carried on the wind when an infected person coughs or sneezes. Just one cough shoots millions of invisible germs into the air like micro cannonballs. I just love finding fresh lungs to infect! Once I'm in, the human body reacts fast. Macrophage attacks me immediately. All-out war with White Blood Cells follows, as they attempt to surround me, while Goblet Cell clogs the pipes with yucky mucus. Sure, I can be tackled using antibiotics, or the BCG vaccine can be injected to prevent my fun. But it's not always successful, so I'll be around for some time yet!

- Discovered: 1882 (Robert Koch)
- Number of people killed: 1.7 million per year (2014)
- BCG vaccine developed: 1921 (Albert Calmette, Camille Guérin)

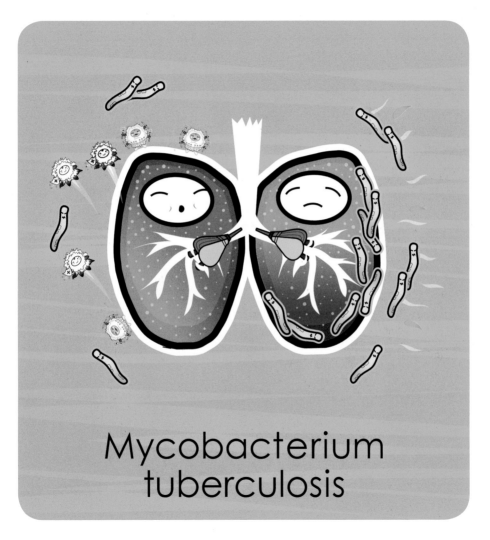

Mycobacterium tuberculosis

Goblet Cell
■ Body Battlers

☀ A special cell that lines the throat, lungs, and gut
☀ Long and thin, it produces mucus that traps bacteria
☀ It helps defend the intestines against wormy invasions

Raise a glass to your gloopy, gunk-making friend! I'm a special type of cell that lines the passageways inside the human body. If I'm good at one thing, it's making slippery, slimy mucus. Gunk-a-liscious!

My slime snares airborne microbes that sneak into the lungs when breathing in air. It engulfs invaders before they have a chance to irritate or infect those delicate windbags. My pal Ciliate Cell then "wafts" the gunk up out of the lungs and into the back of the throat. You'll know we've been at work because you'll feel the "frog" back there. Cough and you may bring up an oyster of ooze! I do the same thing in the gut to keep food slipping and sliding along smoothly. I also stop Body Battler Helminth from hanging onto your gut walls. I win the cup!

● Typical size: 0.0019 in. (0.05 mm)
● Average thickness of mucus layer in nose: 0.0002 in. (0.005 mm)
● Amount of mucus secreted: 20–24 fl. oz. (600–700 mL)/day (mostly from nasal lining)

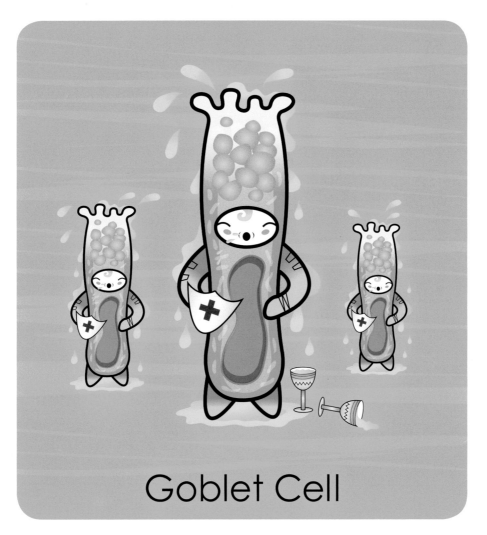

Goblet Cell

Ciliate Cell
■ Body Battlers

☀ A cell with wavy, hairlike projections (cilia) on its surface
☀ Forms part of the lining of the lungs and gut
☀ Moves mucus out of the body, keeping it pathogen free

Oh my gosh! Slender and delicate, I must be the prettiest cell in the human body! My wavy fronds are named cilia, after eyelashes (it's Latin, don't ya know?). I gently bat them to keep a body's innards beautiful and grime free.

Besides White Blood Cells and Macrophage, Goblet Cell and I are vital for a body's immune system. We form the first line of defense against nasty things from the world outside and keep out troublesome Bacteria, Parasite, and dirt. Ours is a onetwo maneuver: Goblet Cell's slime gunks up invaders and I shift them along. I have a great sense of rhythm, waving and waggling in one direction to sweep the soft parts of the body clean. In the outside world, I gobble up all kinds of stuff, including other protists, bacteria, and algae—I'm a real street cleaner!

● Typical length of a cell: 0.0019 in. (0.05mm)
● Typical length of a single cilium: 0.00004–0.00039 in. (0.001–0.01mm)
● Typical thickness of a single cilium: less than 0.00004 in. (0.001mm)

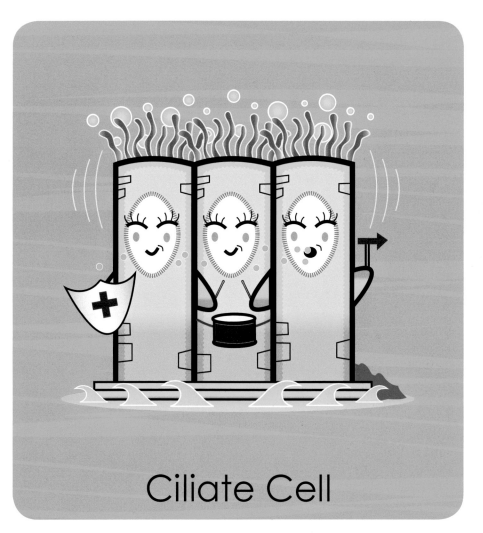

Ciliate Cell

Helminth
■ Body Battlers

❋ Parasites are animals that live on or inside other living things
❋ Helminths are parasitic worms that live inside the body
❋ One-fourth of all people have helminths in their body

A squirmy, wormy bag of fun, I can be a hellish houseguest. I "worm" my way into the human body onboard contaminated food, dirty water, or soil. Once inside, I guzzle on a body's guts and the things passing through.

Although visible to the naked eye at full size, my eggs and young forms are microscopic. I'm skilled at manipulating the immune system to remain undetected. Sometimes this can be helpful, but the toxins I excrete slowly make a person weaker. My types include flatworm flukes, tapeworms, roundworms, and the gruesome Guinea worm, which lives inside a body for a year before its three foot (one meter)-long form emerges from a blister in the skin. And if Goblet Cell is not careful, hookworms might get their hooks into the walls of the intestine to slurp blood.

● Longest tapeworms: 33 ft. (10m) in humans, 98 ft. (30m) in whales
● Biggest bloodguzzler: hookworm, 0.0047–0.0088 fl. oz. (0.14–0.26mL) blood per day
● Most common helminth parasite: roundworm (one billion people infected)

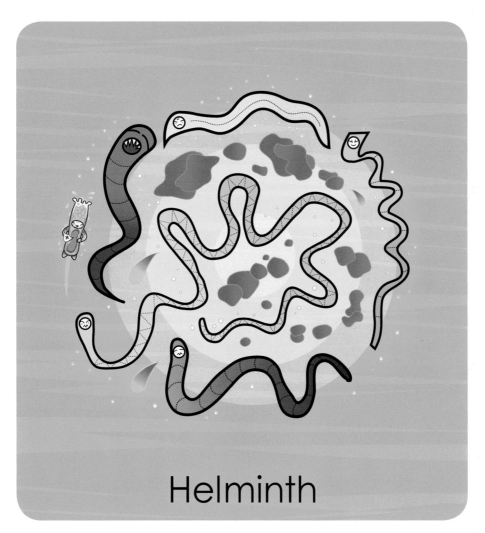

Helminth

Gut Flora
■ Body Battlers

✹ Plays a vital role in the health of the human body
✹ Mainly bacteria, but some fungi, protists, and archaea
✹ Poop transplants help "restock" the body with healthy microbes

Hi, I'm Flora—the friendly bacteria and other microbes that live in the flexible food tubes of every human being. I'm living proof that not all bugs are bad.

Most of a body's microflora are housed in the gut. About two-thirds of human poop is made up of me (which is how doctors discover what lurks in the depths of your insides). I help ferment and break down difficult-to-digest foods, I keep troublesome Bacteria at bay, and I train the immune system to distinguish harmful bugs from helpful ones. It follows that illness is more likely if I'm absent or get out of balance, so take care. Under certain conditions I can turn nasty and might even cause or increase the risk of disease. Want to keep me happy? Stick to a varied diet and avoid eating or drinking too much of any one thing.

● Number of species of microorganism in a healthy body: 10,000
● Number of gut flora cells: 100 trillion (10 times the total number of human cells)
● Number of gut flora genes: about 100 times the number of human genes

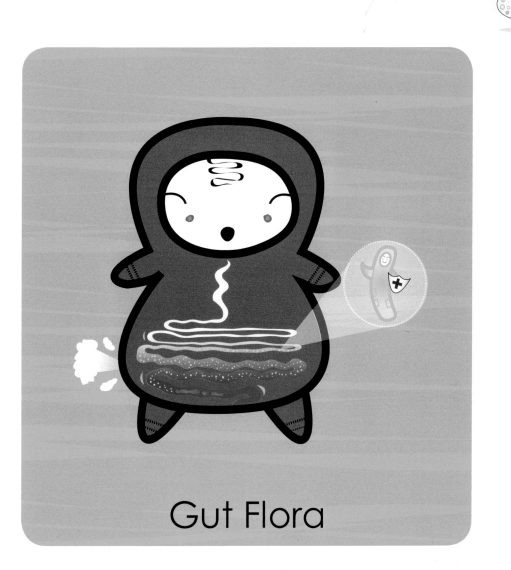

Gut Flora

Streptococcus
■ Body Battlers

✳ A twisted-chain shape of multiple bacteria
✳ Normally lives harmlessly inside your body and on your skin
✳ Can attack the throat to give "strep throat"—and worse

I'm a totally twisted individual with a mean sense of humor. I often play the good guy as an important part of Gut Flora, helping keep a person healthy. I'm even used in producing cheese. But in some of my species, I can be a real busybody of badness!

I'm quick to take advantage of a dip in a body's defenses, blooming to cause a sore throat and swollen tonsils. But that's just for starters. I can also cause pink eye, meningitis, and some forms of pneumonia. I'll let Micro Meanie Impetigo tell you what happens when I get under the skin, but let me into a wound and I'll release a toxin that turns muscle to mush! Yuck! I'm spread by germs in the air—mostly through coughs and sneezes—but I lurk on surfaces, too. Beware of handles on toilets and doors!

● Discovered: 1874 (Theodor Billroth)
● Number of *Streptococcus* species: more than 50
● Cheese made using *Streptococcus*: Emmental

Streptococcus

E. coli

■ Body Battlers

* ✳ AKA *Escherichia coli*, the best-known bacterium on Earth
* ✳ This tiny tyke is part of a body's healthy gut flora
* ✳ Nasty strains give people "stomach bugs"

A villain of vomit, I can be a food-poisoning bacterium that makes people very ill with diarrhea and stomach cramps. I hit young children and the elderly particularly hard.

I live in the gut, often turning up in great quantities in poop. Most of my forms are entirely harmless and have a role to play in helping Gut Flora control the numbers of "bad" Bacteria. I have pathogenic strains, however, and they produce toxins that make people sick, poison the kidneys, and can even kill. I am spread through food and water contaminated with poop. To avoid me, keep food refrigerated, clean your hands before eating, and wash fresh fruit and vegetables. Beware unpasteurized milk and cheese, keep fresh meat and fish separate from other foods, and be sure always to cook them completely.

* ● Discovered: 1885 (Theodor Escherich)
* ● Famous harmful strain: *E. coli* O157:H7
* ● Death toll from 2011 outbreak in Germany: 53 (*E. coli* O104:H4)

E. coli

Chapter 4
Micro Meanies

Shudder, shiver, and shake in your boots, for here are the hostile horrors of the microscopic world. The Micro Meanies are "pathogens"—bugs that bring sickness and disease. They include the African assassinator Ebola Virus, kitty-bound killer *Toxoplasma gondii*, heartless Black Death, and grim skin infesters Ringworm, Impetigo, and Scabies. The real frightener, however, is Antimicrobial Resistance. This terror blocks the best antibiotic drugs. Thanks to Bacteria's ace ability to swap pieces of drug-resistant DNA (even between species), Antimicrobial Resistance leaves us helpless in the face of invaders.

Black Death

Flu Virus

Ebola Virus

Toxoplasma gondii

Ringworm

Impetigo

Scabies

Antimicrobial Resistance

Black Death
■ Micro Meanies

✳ A medieval pandemic also known as the bubonic plague
✳ The disease is caused by the bacterium *Yersinia pestis*
✳ It is spread by fleas living on rats and other rodents

Bring out your dead! Bring out your dead! I was a medieval mass murderer. Wherever I visited in the 1300s, the townsfolk dropped like flies. It was not pleasant for the peasants, and the high and mighty didn't escape either!

I spread like wildfire from China, carried by rodent fleas. Once I got into the lungs, I went airborne. The damage I caused! Pus-filled lumps grew in the groin and armpits, then black spots spread across the skin. Fever and vomiting blood came next, followed by death two to eight days later. I killed one in five of the world's population and half of all the people in Europe. I even triggered widespread famine, having left too few workers to harvest crops. I'm still around today, but thanks to better health, hygiene, and antibiotics, I'm kept at bay . . . for now!

● Discovery of *Yersinia pestis*: 1894 (Alexandre Yersin)
● Black Death body count: 75–200 million people (1346–1353)
● Modern death toll: 32 (Madagascar, 2013)

Black Death

Flu Virus
Micro Meanies

✳ An airborne infection that attacks nose, throat, and lungs
✳ Influenza viruses are made inactive by soap—start washing!
✳ Some forms of bird flu and swine flu can spread to humans

Do not underestimate me. You may think of me as winter sniffles, a thumping headache, and a big red nose, but I am pure evil, a merciless serial slaughterer. *Mwahahaha!*

Tens of millions of people catch a dose of me each year. I carry off the weak and sick, but can also suddenly attack and kill strong and healthy types. Because I travel on the air, it's incredibly easy for me to pass from person to person. My tiny virus spheres bristle with curiously shaped chemicals that act as keys, allowing me to walk straight through Cell's front door. I spread rapidly, hijacking Cell's mechanisms to make new copies of myself. Sure, there are flu vaccines that allow a body to stockpile "antibody" defenses, which can be used against me when I hit at full strength. But, hey, I mutate easily, and those vaccines are quickly outwitted.

● Typical size of influenza virus: 0.000003–0.000008 in. (0.00008–0.00012mm)
● Most killed in flu outbreak: 50–100 million (Spanish flu pandemic,1918)
● Average death toll: 250,000–500,000 per year

Flu Virus

Ebola Virus
Micro Meanies

☀ Hemorrhagic fever syndrome caused by *Filoviridae* viruses
☀ Spread via the body fluids and dirty linen of infected people
☀ This deadly virus is found in bat and monkey bushmeat

A rainforest rotter, I'm a hot zone hit man. Lurking in the tropical regions of Africa, I'm a truly horrible little virus capable of killing 90 percent of the people I infect.

I start by causing flu-like headaches, fevers, achy limbs, and a sore throat. This general illness soon progresses to stomach pain and spouting from both ends. Then, as the walls of tiny blood vessels start to separate, there's bleeding into the eyeballs and leakage from the inside (hemorrhage). Once the blood circulation system fails to work properly, it's all over. There's no known cure.
I am so infectious that doctors must wear HAZMAT suits and burn dirty bedding to avoid contagion. I may be frighteningly lethal, but because I'm not an airborne disease, I'm far less destructive than my cousin Flu Virus.

● First recorded outbreak: 1976 (Ebola River, Democratic Republic of Congo)
● Incubation period: 2–21 days
● Most recent outbreak: 2014 (Liberia, Guinea, Sierra Leone, Nigeria, Mali)

Ebola Virus

Toxoplasma gondii

Micro Meanies

✳ A parasite that causes a condition called toxoplasmosis
✳ It is serious in unborn children and those with weak defenses
✳ May be present in one-third of the world's population

A master of mind control, I'm a single-celled lurker found lodging in skin, muscle tissue, lymph nodes, and other nervous tissue. Cats are the purrr-fect hosts for me, but I'll take any warm-blooded animal—I'm not picky.

I'm transmitted by anything contaminated with cat poop —food, water, or soil—and by undercooked meat. Once I get inside the body, I hide from the immune system inside a thin-walled bubble called a cyst. I invade Macrophage and Cell and even burrow into the brain. Like all parasites, I alter my host's behavior to suit my own ends. I sprinkle the brain with chemicals that encourage bravery so that a mouse will lose its fear of cats . . . to its peril. (How else to find my way into the cat and so reach my adult stage?) Just think of the psycho effect I might be having on you!

● Discovered: 1908 (Charles Nicolle and Louis Manceaux)
● Typical size of *Toxoplasma* parasite: 0.0002 in. (0.005mm)
● Typical size of infectious "oocysts" in cat poop: 0.00039 in. (0.01mm)

Toxoplasma gondii

Ringworm
■ Micro Meanies

✴ Fungal infection of the upper layers of the skin
✴ Passed on by touching, by sharing towels, and by pets
✴ Causes silvery or red rings on the surface of the skin

The first of the brothers grim—the top three skin infections—I love a practical joke. I'm called Ringworm, but actually I'm a fungus! Ha ha, tricked ya! I spread from person to person via spores that find their way under the skin through cuts and cracks. Then I pull my best trick, making itchy, red rings on the skin. You guessed it—that's where I get my name!

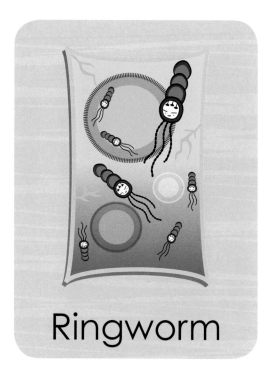

Ringworm

● Fungus that causes ringworm: *Tinea corporis*
● Incubation period: 4–10 days
● Diameter of round pink patches: 0.5–1 in. (12–25mm)

Impetigo

Micro Meanies

* Skin complaint caused by the *Streptococcus* bacterium
* Causes itchy sores and blisters on the skin
* Passed on by skin contact and sharing clothes or towels

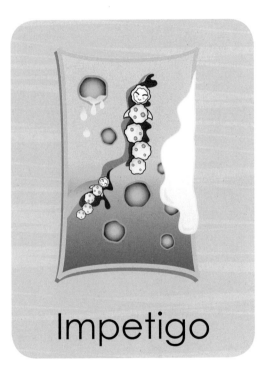

Impetigo

Caused by Body Battler *Streptococcus*, I'm grim brother number two. I break in through cuts, grazes, and cracks in dry skin and can be treated using bacteria-killing antibiotic cream. I can be either bulbous or (slightly less gruesome and more frequent) nonbulbous. No doubt you've guessed that my bulbous version comes with bubbling, pus-filled carbuncles. Nice!

● Bacteria that cause impetigo: *Staphylococcus aureus*; *Streptococcus pyogenes*
● Incubation period: 1–3 days (*Streptococcus*); 4–10 days (*Staphylococcus*)
● Number of people affected by impetigo: 140 million per year

Scabies
Micro Meanies

✳ A skin infestation caused by the tiny *Sarcoptes scabiei* mite
✳ It is passed on through skin-on-skin contact
✳ This beastly burrower causes an itchy, burning rash

Am I not the mightiest of the minimites? Don't my six legs and crazy stray hairs freak you out? Let me hang out a little longer and I'll really get under your skin! I'm a total animal when compared with my fellow brothers grim, Ringworm and Impetigo. You see, although I'm microscopic, I'm related to spiders and scorpions.

My trick is to burrow beneath the top layer of the skin and lay eggs. Not only does this make the skin red and lumpy, but it itches like crazy. This rash (which I can also make into yucky pus-filled lumps) is caused by an allergic reaction to my poop. I feed on dead skin cells—I totally "dig" them (get it?). I'm too small to see, but you will definitely feel me. And once I'm in, I have a nasty habit of leaving the door open for Ringworm and Impetigo.

● Lifespan of scabies mite: 2–3 days (in clothing)
● Record scabies infestation: 3,859 people (1989; Kildare, Montana)
● Number of people affected by scabies: 100 million per year

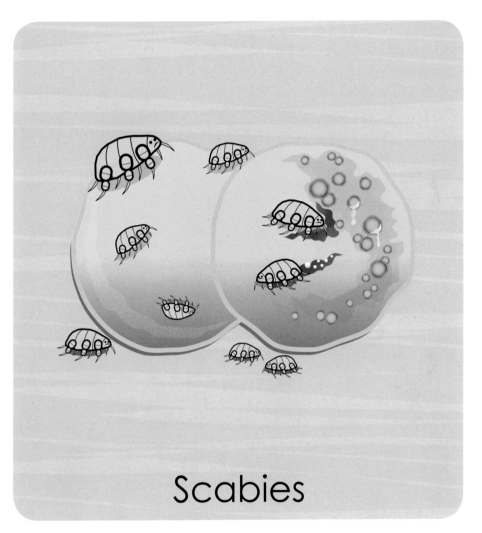

Scabies

Antimicrobial Resistance

Micro Meanies

- ✳ When microorganisms fight back against antibiotics
- ✳ This creates a host of infections that are harder to treat
- ✳ Natural enemies include hand washing and good hygiene

Mighty creator of the "superbug," I scoff in the face of medicine. Full of spite and ready to fight, I've got doctors running scared. How can scientists treat nasty diseases caused by bacteria, fungi, parasites, and viruses in the face of bugs that develop resistance to medicine?

Antimicrobials (such as antibiotics) may be "wonder drugs" of the modern age, but they have a weak spot. In killing disease-carrying pathogens, they weed out the weak ones first, leaving the field clear for beefed-up bugs. It's a case of what doesn't kill them makes them stronger! I'm a particular problem in hospitals, where widespread use of antimicrobials opens the door to superstrength antibiotic-resistant bugs such as *Clostridium difficile* and MRSA.

- ● MRSA: methicillin-resistant *Staphylococcus aureus*
- ● Number of major new antibiotics developed in past 30 years: 0
- ● AMR-bacteria-related deaths: 23,000 per year (U.S.); 25,000 per year (Europe)

Antimicrobial Resistance

Chapter 5
Hardcore Herd

The Hardcore Herd loves all the things that your body can't take—excess heat, extreme cold, nuclear radiation, caustic acid, and too much salt. In fact, these guys can't get enough, which is why they are called "extremophiles." The word means "extreme-loving." These organisms are tolerant of extreme and hostile environments that would kill most other living things. They can live buried under Antarctic ice, on scalding-hot hydrothermal vents, or even in the seabed beneath miles of seawater. Scientists think that life on Earth may have begun with these ancient creatures. Do you dare enter the extreme zone?

Conan the Bacterium

Cryophile

Thermophile

Acidophile

Halophile

Slime Mold

Conan the Bacterium

Hardcore Herd

✳ This bacterium is resistant to damage by radiation
✳ Discovered when a can of meat spoiled despite being sterilized
✳ This hardcore hero is also known as *Deinococcus radiodurans*

There's no doubt about it, I'm a superbug. Sure, plenty of bacteria are resistant to radiation, but none are as hard as me. I've even been crowned the World's Toughest Bacterium by the *Guinness Book of World Records*.

Drought? Easy. Starvation? A cinch. Acid attack? Don't make me laugh! Radiation? I can take levels 1,000 times greater than a human being can. What's my secret? I have multiple backup copies of my genes. It means I always have a copy of a gene that is damage free. Humans have just one or two copies—no wonder you're so fragile! With my staying power, I could help clean up radioactive spills or treat sewage on long space missions. Tough stuff, indeed!

● Discovered: 1956 (Arthur W. Anderson)
● Genome sequenced: 1999 (TIGR, Maryland)
● Number of genes: more than 3,000

Conan the Bacterium

Cryophile
Hardcore Herd

✳ A microorganism that loves the cold
✳ Lives in soil and ice in high places, polar regions, and deep seas
✳ Could be the kind of life form that shelters on other planets

Some like it hot, but I like it chilly. I'm one cool critter (say *cry-oh-file*) that hangs out where the temperature is rarely above freezing. I'm found in the Arctic, Antarctica, and as far as two miles (3km) beneath the Greenland ice sheet.

Freezing is usually fatal for living things. This is because water that turns to ice inside a cell busts the delicate membrane that keeps the cell together. Living tissues also tend to go as hard as bones (think of meat after it's been in your freezer at home). I combat these effects by storing hard-to-freeze fats in my membranes and also by being incredibly sluggish. I grow ever so slowly, dividing just a handful of times a year. Scientists use my proteins in cold-water detergents and antifreezes in order to keep things going at low temperatures.

● Temperature range of cryophiles: −4–50 °F (−20–10 °C)
● Low-temperature survival record: −13 °F (−25 °C) (*Planococcus halocryophilus*)
● Experimental cryophile biogas digester: 52–79 gal. (200–300L) of methane per day

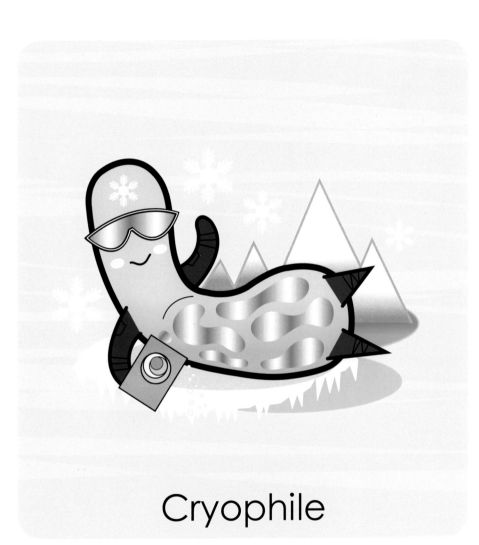

Cryophile

Thermophile
Hardcore Herd

✳ This heat-loving organism can stand intense heat
✳ Discovered in hot springs in Yellowstone National Park
✳ Thermophiles were among the earliest life forms on Earth

Turn up the heat—I like it hot, hot, hot! I hang out in and around volcanoes. There's nothing I like better than taking a dip in a boiling hot spring. Cooking!

I also live deep under the oceans around hydrothermal vents—the scalding "black smokers" that pump out heat and minerals. Far from the Sun's rays, I take my food and energy from the vent itself—this may be how life on Earth began. You humans are pathetic, with proteins that only operate correctly at 98.6 °F (37 °C). The key lies in being very careful to keep hot water away from your vitals. I have a number of chemical tricks to avoid turning into a boiled egg. My heat-resistant enzymes are used in the polymerase chain reaction (PCR)—a process used to make copies of DNA. Scientists may use me in future industrial processes.

● Discovered: 1965 (Thomas D. Brock)
● Temperature range of thermophiles: 113–252 °F (45–122 °C)
● High-temperature survival record: 252 °F (122 °C) (*Methanopyrus kandleri*)

Thermophile

Acidophile
Hardcore Herd

✹ Corrosive-crazy organism that tolerates acid environments
✹ Lives in volcanic hot springs and hydrothermal vents
✹ Many acidophiles are also thermophiles and halophiles

I love to float around in battery acid. This may be a harsh environment but, unlike the acid, I'm not bitter! I'm tolerant of corrosive zones because I'm extremely efficient at pumping harmful, positively charged protons out of the liquids surrounding my cells. Scientists use me to speed up the extraction of metals from their ores and to provide acid-resistant enzymes.

Acidophile

● Acidity level of human body: pH 7.35–7.45
● pH of battery acid: 1.0
● Record acid tolerance: pH –0.06 (*Picrophilus* sp.)

Halophile

Hardcore Herd

- ✳ Brine-loving bacterium that lives in harsh salty environments
- ✳ Any place that is five times saltier than the sea is its home
- ✳ Keeps its chemical balance just right to prevent drying out

Halophile

A crusty salt fiend, I'm built to withstand salt levels almost ten times greater than seawater without drying out or getting thirsty. I actually *need* high levels of salt to survive. I live in the briny Dead Sea and the Great Salt Lake. I tint some brackish waters bright pink and orange. I'm used to make lip-licking snacks such as soy sauce and sauerkraut. Smackeroo!

- ● Salt levels of seawater: 3.5% (by volume)
- ● Halophile salt range: 20–30% salt
- ● World's largest salt lake: 4,086 sq. mi. (10,582km²) (Salar de Uyuni, Bolivia)

Slime Mold
Hardcore Herd

✴ Single-celled marvel that feeds on bacteria, yeast, and fungi
✴ Slime molds are protists, not fungi (despite the name)
✴ A "smart" protist that joins a network to hunt down food

I'm a brainless wonder—a creeping, quivery mass that rampages (slowly) in search of food. You'll see my blubbery networks growing on rotting logs and leaf mold or spilling out of trash cans, gutters, and blocked drains.

There are two types of slimers. A "plasmodial" slime mold is one great big cell—the world's largest—filled with multiple nuclei. "Cellular" slime molds are colonies made of many individual cells that act as one. My fave food is bacteria. That yummy goo is all I live for. When grub gets scarce, cellular molds do something unbelievable—they join forces and turn into a slug-like creature. The slug slithers up high and "fruiting bodies" bud out of its back. These release spores, which drift off on the wind to make new slimy generations. Smart stuff indeed.

- Discovery of dog vomit slime mold: 1727 (Jean Marchant)
- Speed of growth in strand of plasmodial slime mold: 0.05 in./s (1.35mm/s)
- Heaviest slime mold: 1 oz. (30g)

Slime Mold

Chapter 6
Bug Buddies

When you read about "microbes," if you think "uggy bugs," you're only getting half of the story. Yes, microbugs can invade your body and make you ill—that's why you wash your hands before you eat and clean cuts and scrapes. But many of these tiny tots are terrific! As primary producers, they underpin the planet's food chains, providing nosh for every other living thing. Microbes also clean up after humans. Feeding on things that have died, they remove waste and recycle essential chemicals. And without soil microbes, plants couldn't take up nutrients and wouldn't grow. Now you know who to blame for your green vegetables!

Paramecium

Thermus aquaticus

Bacteriophage

Vaccine

Probiotics

Penicillium

Cyanobacteria

Mycelium

Soil Bacteria

Yeast

Yogurt

Paramecium
■ Bug Buddies

☀ A single-celled, slipper-shaped protist with cilia
☀ "Organelles" inside this critter carry out essential life functions
☀ Avoids objects by bumping into them and changing direction

I am a peace-loving protist. I blunder around in lakes, streams, ponds, and puddles, slurping up Bacteria and Yeast. I was one of the first minibeasts to be found—if you've got sharp eyes, you might spot me as a tiny speck, but to see me at my best you need a microscope.

I have a lovely bristly coat made of short hairs called cilia. When I wish to move from place to place, I simply wiggle them. I also waft them to direct food toward the tiny pore that serves as my mouth. I'm a total teacher's pet—I'm used in the classroom to study Protists' behavior (my escape tactics are infamous) and in the laboratory for genetic research. My biggest enemy is the fearsome carnivorous *Didinium*, another ciliate. It's only half my size but can swallow me whole. Gulp!

●   Named: 1718 (Louis Joblot)
●   Typical size: 0.0019–0.13 in. (0.05–0.33mm); *Didinium*, up to 0.00059 in. (0.015mm)
●   Paramecium top speed: 12 body lengths per second

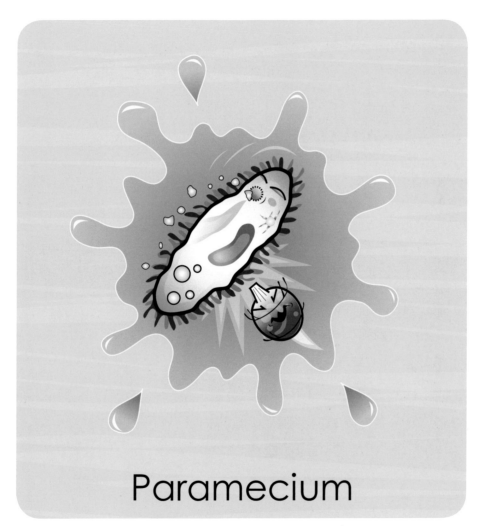

Paramecium

Thermus aquaticus
Bug Buddies

* Rod-shaped, heat-loving bacterium found in thermal springs
* Proves that life can survive in harsh environments
* Important source of heat-stable enzymes (e.g. *Taq* polymerase)

Dressed in a toga and shower cap, I hang out in thermal springs—the muddy baths and hot bubbly mineral waters that rise from deep inside Earth. I was discovered in the Lower Geyser Basin in Yellowstone National Park, where I live off sulfur-rich chemicals.

Scientists were surprised to find me in places topping 158 °F (70 °C), since proteins—essential life chemicals produced in cells—usually "denature" when heated. This is what makes egg proteins go white and solidify when cooked. My enzymes (proteins) are heat-toughened, and one in particular—*Taq* polymerase—is used in the polymerase chain reaction (PCR) for copying DNA in genetics labs. It is used in forensic labs, to copy DNA from tiny samples found at crime scenes to get a "DNA fingerprint" of suspects.

● Discovered: 1969 (Thomas D. Brock)
● Temperature range: 131–176 °F (55– 80 °C)
● Invention of PCR: 1983 (Kary Mullis)

Thermus aquaticus

Bacteriophage
Bug Buddies

✳ This viral devourer attacks and infects bacterial cells
✳ Bacteria-killers are found wherever there are bacteria
✳ Can be used as an alternative to antibiotics

I am a tiny assassin who targets bacteria. I'm little known, but as far back as the 1890s scientists noticed that something invisible to their microscopes knocked out bacteria. The unidentified nanohero was yours truly!

Like all viruses, I lack the means to reproduce and multiply, so I hijack cells and trick them into replicating my DNA. Compared with me, a bacterium is vast, but nothing fazes this phage! I latch on, drill through a bacterium's surface, and inject my DNA. Once enough copies of me have been made, I explode out of the cell and go looking for more victims. I can destroy multidrug-resistant bugs, help skin grafts bind without infection, and kill off bacteria that spoil food. Genetic engineers use me to deliver their specially designed strips of DNA into a bacterium's genome.

● Discovered: 1915 (Frederick W. Twort) and 1917 (Félix d'Hérelle)
● Discovery of *E. coli*-killing bacteriophage: 1950 (Esther Lederberg)
● Richest bacteriophage source: 25.6 billion per fl. oz (900 million per ml) (seawater)

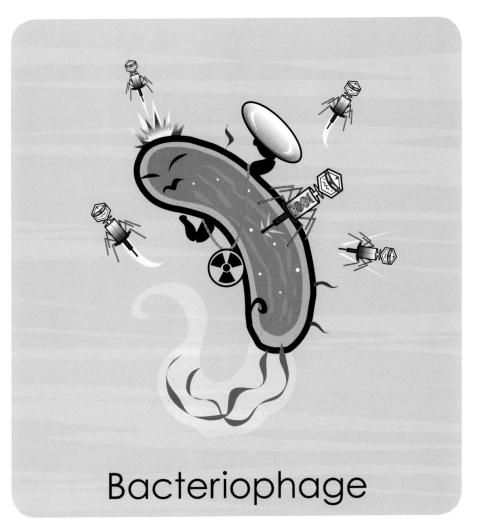

Bacteriophage

Vaccine
■ Bug Buddies

☀ A weakened form of a pathogen
☀ It trains the body's immune system to "remember" an invader
☀ Vaccines prevent disease or make it less serious

I'll beef up a body's defenses to diseases by giving its immune system the chance to practice on a lower-strength bad guy. I can be an inactivated bug (flu vaccine) or live, but weakened, bug (TB vaccine). I have punted smallpox into the past and almost have polio licked. I also help target cholera, bubonic plague, Ebola, measles, mumps, rubella, rabies . . . and many more!

Vaccine

● First vaccine: 1798 (smallpox; Edward Jenner)
● Reduction in whooping cough (pertussis) deaths due to vaccine: over 99% (U.S.)
● First testing of experimental Ebola vaccine: 2014

Probiotics
Bug Buddies

* These "good bacteria" provide health benefits
* Can replace normal gut flora following a course of antibiotics
* "Live" yogurts should contain probiotic active cultures

Probiotics

We are a health-giving bunch who keep your insides working. Gut bacteria are important for helping digestion, producing vitamins, and fighting those gut Micro Meanies that make you sick. We have fancy names like *Bifidobacteria* and *Lactobacillus bulgaricus*.You'll find us in yogurts and cheeses, so if you like eating those, go for it!

- *Bifidobacterium* discovered: 1924 (Sigurd Orla-Jensen)
- Value of probiotics market: $16 billion
- Number of bacteria in gut: 100 trillion

Penicillium

■ Bug Buddies

✳ Blue or green mold that causes fruit and veggie decay
✳ It produces a bacteria-busting antibiotic—penicillin
✳ Penicillin is the world's most widely used antibiotic drug

I am a common type of moldy fungus. My spores drift around in dust and air, and I grow on almost any surface. You'll know me as the fuzzy blue bloom that grows on food.

I'm not all bad—some of my varieties are used to make tasty blue cheeses. Best of all, I produce the wonder drug penicillin. Discovered just in time for use in World War II, it stopped bacterial infections from poisoning the blood of wounded soldiers, saving countless lives. As penicillin, I am a chemical that stops bacteria building their cell walls, so they can't reproduce or cause sickness-making infections. I am a "broad-spectrum" antibiotic, which means that I am effective against many types of bacteria. However, overusing my drugs—or failing to finish a prescribed course—opens the door to Antimicrobial Resistance.

● Penicillin discovered: 1929 (Alexander Fleming)
● Number of *Penicillium* species: more than 300
● Species used to make penicillin: *Penicillium chrysogenum*

Penicillium

Cyanobacteria
Bug Buddies

☀ This photosynthesizing bacteria lives mostly in soil and water
☀ Long, long ago, it filled Earth's atmosphere with oxygen
☀ Some incorrectly call it "blue-green algae"

We were the first living things to capture energy from the Sun and use it to convert carbon dioxide into sugary food. We are the ancestors of all green things—a plant's "chloroplasts" are basically cyanobacteria.

Before we arrived on the scene, Earth's atmosphere was a choking mix of toxic gases. We filled it with oxygen—you could say that we were a breath of fresh air for the planet! We have a claim on the title of World's Most Successful Living Thing—we are the most diverse group and we range across all habitats. We may be old, but we have one flagellum on the future—*Spirulina* could feed astronauts on long-range space voyages. Right now we're helping develop new green power sources based on artificial photosynthesis. You can't get greener than blue-green!

● Evolution of photosynthesis: more than 3.7 billion years ago
● Some species "fix" atmospheric nitrogen for use by plants
● Algae-based fuels supplement diesel, gasoline, and jet fuel

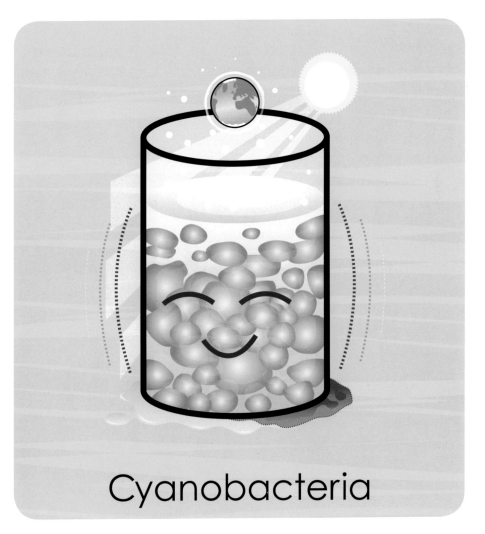

Cyanobacteria

Mycelium
Bug Buddies

✳ Dark, mysterious "body" part of a fungus that lives underground
✳ Made up of sheets of very fine fibers
✳ Its "fruiting bodies" (mushrooms) grow above ground

I'm an undergrounder who runs a complex murky web. In the dark, moist soil, I spread out my threadlike filament fingers, drawing up nutrients and breaking down organic matter. I am a total rotter! I create new soil, help plants take up vital nutrients through their roots, and turn your kitchen and yard waste into compost. I can even clean up land contaminated by gasoline and pesticides!

Mycelium

● Largest living thing: *Armillaria solidipes* "Humongous Fungus" (Oregon)
● Size: covers 3.2 sq. mi. (8.4km²)
● Age: about 2,400 years old

Soil Bacteria
Bug Buddies

* Mini marvels that make the soil habitable for plant life
* They turn inorganic matter into plant food
* Soil bacteria occur in nitrogen-fixing root nodules

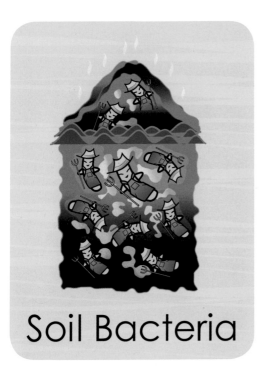

Soil Bacteria

We bacterial farmers are essential for all living things taking nutrients from the ground. Mostly we break down and recycle organic matter—check out that "earthy" compost smell! Some of us "fix" nitrogen in the soil—plants can't get this essential chemical any other way. Others are natural insecticides or fungicides. We kill crop-damaging bugs. We totally "dig" it!

● Number of bacteria in a teaspoonful of soil: 100 million–3 billion
● Botulin poisoning: caused by soil bacterium *Clostridium botulinum*
● Wet, poorly drained soils encourage toxic anaerobic soil bacteria

Yeast
■ Bug Buddies

❋ A fungus that converts sugar into carbon dioxide and alcohol
❋ This single-celled belcher is used in baking and beer making
❋ Some types cause uncomfortable yeast infections

Hic! I'm the jolliest fungus—a gassy guy who puts the bubbles into beer and makes cakes and bread rise to the occasion. It's (almost) always party time when I'm around!

A naturally occurring beastie, I'm commonly found on the skins of grapes. When they are crushed, I begin to feast on their sugary pulp, turning the juice fizzy and alcoholic. I'm also added to bread dough and left to "prove" somewhere warm. Working away in the dark, I belch out bubbles of carbon dioxide, filling the bread with gas. This is what makes it rise and stay soft and fluffy as it bakes. I come into my own as a model eukaryote for genetic research, for use in microbial fuel cells, and also as a producer of biofuel. Well, it's the "yeast" I can do!

● Number of yeast species: more than 500
● Pathogenic yeast: *Candida* (causes "yeast" infections)
● Probiotic yeast: *Saccharomyces boulardii* (reduces risk of diarrhea)

Yeast

Yogurt
Bug Buddies

✳ Bacteria called "yogurt cultures" are used to make yogurt
✳ Fermented in warm milk, these bacteria produce a tangy acid
✳ It's an ancient food of nomadic yak herders of central Asia

Yo—you can call me Gurtie! I'm a delicious soft gloop of fermented milk and "good" bacteria. Sound tempting? Try me and you'll find I'm smooth, suave, and "cultured."

My invention allowed herders to carry a nutritious food across the plains while keeping it fresh. The first stage of making me is to heat milk to around 176 °F (80 °C). This kills off Micro Meanies in the cow juice and favors the culture of added *Lactobacillus* and *Streptococcus* bacteria. These ferment lactose in the milk to produce lactic acid, which gives me a zesty tang. I contain protein, calcium, and vitamins. And because the lactose is converted, I help people who are lactose intolerant (unable to digest lactose in milk). If I still contain "live" bacteria, I become probiotic and help restock the gut with good bacteria.

● Discovery of *Lactobacillus delbrueckii* ssp. *bulgaricus*: 1905 (Stamen Grigorov)
● Boiling or straining the milk produces thicker yogurt
● Yogurt and honey: AKA "the food of the gods"

Yogurt

Index

Pages that show characters are in **bold**

Glossary

AIDS A disease caused by the HIV virus. It attacks the body's immune system. AIDS stands for "acquired immune deficiency syndrome."

Algae Eukaryote autotrophs that take energy from the Sun. Algae range from single-celled microorganisms to multicelled seaweeds.

Amoeba A tiny, single-celled eukaryote that can change its shape. Amoebas are mostly protists but can also be fungi, algae, and animals.

Antibiotics Drugs designed to kill microbes or stop them from growing.

Antibody A special protein produced by the body that latches on to bacteria and viruses, "flagging" them as invaders for the immune system to deal with.

Bioluminescent Describes living things that can produce light. A number of marine animals and insects can do this.

Chemosynthesis The ability of living things to make the essential chemicals for life using energy from chemical reactions.

Chloroplasts Tiny little organelles inside a plant cell that harvest energy from sunlight. Originally they were photosynthesising cyanobacteria.

Contagion The spread of a disease from one person to another. A disease that is easily transmitted is contagious.

Contamination The addition of a pathogen or poison to make something unhealthy.

Cytoplasm The watery fluid that fills a cell.

Denature To destroy the properties of a biological chemical that make it useful, usually by heat or acidity.

DNA A life chemical, twisted into a double-stranded spiral, which holds the genetic instructions for building and running a living thing. DNA stands for "deoxyribonucleic acid."

Enzyme A nonliving chemical that helps control the rate of processes inside cells and the bodies of living things.

Eukaryote A living thing whose cells store their DNA in a central nucleus. Eukaryotes include single-celled and multicellular organisms.

Fungi A major kingdom of living spore-producing organisms. The kingdom includes molds, yeast, and mushrooms.

Gene Short length of DNA that contains chemical instructions on how to build and run a living thing.

Genome The entire set of genes and non-coding DNA belonging to a living thing.

HAZMAT suit HAZMAT is short for "hazardous materials." A HAZMAT suit keeps people safe from contagious microorganisms. It is worn by scientists and medical workers when working with dangerous pathogens.

Hot spring Natural mineral water that bubbles up to the surface in volcanic regions.

Hydrothermal vent A "chimney" on the seabed from which heated mineral water flows.

Immunity The ability to resist infection by pathogenic microorganisms.

Infectious Describes something that is capable of being passed from one person to another (such as a disease).

Microbe A nonscientific term for a microscopic living thing, often used to mean "germ."

Molecule A substance made from two or more atoms bonded together and that gets involved in chemical reactions.

Monocyte The largest white blood cell and part of the body's immune system.

Nucleus The central part of a eukaryotic cell, where DNA is stored.

Organelle A specialized structure within a cell; the chloroplasts in plant cells or mitochondria inside animal cells, for example.

Oxidize To combine chemically with oxygen.

Glossary

Parasite An organism that lives in or on another different living thing, benefitting at the host's expense.

Pasteurize To kill microbes through heat. Many foods, such as milk and wine, are pasteurized.

Pathogen A microorganism that can cause disease.

pH A measure of the acidity of any substance. The lower the pH, the more acidic something is.

Photosynthesis The ability of a living thing to make the essential chemicals for life using energy from sunlight.

Polymer A substance made from many long molecules of the same kind. Most plastics are polymers.

Prokaryote A living thing whose cells have no central nucleus. All prokaryotes are single-celled microorganisms.

Protein Nonliving chemical that carries out essential life processes inside living things. Enzymes and RNA are examples of proteins.

Proton A heavy, positively changed subatomic particle found in the nucleus of an atom.

Quorum sensing A system based on "signal" chemicals and "receptors," used by bacteria to sense their numbers and coordinate their actions.

Radiation Strictly called "radioactivity," this involves energetic particles or a zap of energy that comes shooting out of an atomic nucleus when it breaks apart. Radioactivity can damage DNA.

RNA An important life chemical that carries out many functions in the cell, including copying DNA. It stands for "ribonucleic acid."

Toxin A poison or venom produced by a living thing. When produced by microorganisms in the body, it can cause disease.